THE ALMIGHTY

Volume- 1

A BOOK IN THE GENRE OF POETRY

PREM AGARWAL

ZORBA BOOKS

ZORBA BOOKS

Publishing Services in India by Zorba Books, 2019

Website: www.zorbabooks.com
Email: info@zorbabooks.com

Copyright © Prem Agarwal

Printbook ISBN 978-93-88497-90-9
E-book ISBN 978-81-943110-2-7

Zorba Books Pvt. Ltd. (opc)
Gurgaon, INDIA

FOREWORD

The moment of truth.... the bank of Hooghly River, district Howrah at the other bank at a distance, howrah bridge far away in the right as if will never vanish how far it may be and in the back are the underground Fort William on a fairly large expanse, not very far in the right the Garden of Eden.... sorry .... the Eden Gardens, the governor house, the red road and not very far in the left the race course, the legendary Victoria Memorial with its enchanting garden and the sprawling maidan and I at my tender age of 17, sitting on this bank on a victorian seat looking at the flow of this river, a sort of short memorial nearby with a roundabout staircase leading to its black circled top and on the left of my back not very far is a lonely, imposing memorial with its roman-type huge pillars and on the backdrop of this all I shut my eyes focussing on the flow and the moment of truth struck and took me over when I was unwittingly introduced to the dynamics of the apparent universe and to its beyond and since that moment and till now I remain indebted to Calcutta but if I was to be overwhelmed by this city then why I was not born to a Bengali mom, then the world could not have been formed without its inconsistencies, but the truth of the moment was very stark and consistent, the dual purpose of the apparent universe is to produce energy at the core of its stars and to create the steady flow of true joy in each and every unit of the apparent universe by using the streak of light and the tryst of relativity.

In some moments I shall cease to exist and in the distant some moments the whole apparent universe will cease to exist as the Almighty will fall into his blissful slumber settled calmly into his infinite body of space, the energy-less, the matter-less, the motion-less, the gravity-less and the soul of the Almighty will turn into a

complete rest, the deathly inactivity and the mind of the Almighty will return and freeze and stay put into the subconscious of the Almighty.

Dear reader I feel pleasure in forwarding this book to you, I take leave for now.

Oct-2019
NCR, Delhi

Prem Agarwal

A FEW WORDS ABOUT THE AUTHOR

It has been a dream of this Poet to get his creative works published and Zorba Books took the lead to support and publish his Ist book – THE ALMIGHTY - Vol. 1.

As of now, the poet has the inclination to create a total of 5 volumes of THE ALMIGHTY - currently he is engaged in creating the 2nd volume of - THE ALMIGHTY - for which he is hopeful to accomplish in 2 years time.

We at Zorba Books wish him success in his endeavor. The genre of poetry stands to gain by his contributions.

Oct-2019
NCR- Delhi

Zorba Books

PREFACE & ACKNOWLEDGEMENTS

The moon is enhanced and I become sensuous and I play the host and moon takes the charge and reaches the zenith of its splendour and kisses my heart, I being the host, I press on further and hold the moon tightly and relish its charm and savor its fire and endure its pass and satiated by the invading full moon I tell it to go away and not to return again as it reduces slowly and vanishes behind a naught only to reappear and start creating joy again and when it is no more and its shine is gone its enchantment lingers on......

Belonging to an unimportant background but grown into the swift & gutsy, balmy, energizing and inspiring southern winds and into the proximity of the Mullick - Kothi with its enchanting garden on an enclosed acres & acres of expanse and accessibility to the winds from the south and to an eye-view of the kothi and its garden from the north available freely through some vantage points of the place of my residence, I was brought up in the vicinity of the steadfast Howrah-Bridge serving to the gateway to the east the iconic Howrah-Station, the bustling pachmathamore, the waning but charming Rajbaris-Thakurbaris, the sacred Belurmath, the mystical Dakneswar-temple and near to its maingate an eccentric but sturdy and ever-alert shoe-keeper, a lame and one leg amputated person to whom, somehow, am not able to clear out from my memory, the breathtaking botanical garden, somehow, is able to hide itself from the common purview, the alluring Ballyganj-Lake, the aforesaid few among many-many fascinating others, I acknowledge my deep-seated respect for the city of Calcutta and its insight-rich and intelligence-oriented people with natural inclination for art and music.

I dedicate this book to Vanshika, while nearing to her teen, had shown courage when she approached a renowned writer, tugging the said writer's book in her hand to get his autograph, and blurted: Hi-Sir, my Nana is also a nature-lover as you are and he is a writer too!

This book could not have been possible without the deft efforts of the team at Zorba Books and I am thankful to them and specially to Mr. Sunil for his uninterrupted support and to Ms Komal by whom I was benefitted by her spontaneity and by her diligence.

Oct-2019
NCR, Delhi

PREM AGARWAL

CONTENTS

PART-II

BATCH-I , PART -1

1. THE ALMIGHTY - I   (60)

.... THE EARTH AND THE MANKIND ....   (6)

- Adrift and rudderless in your lap and pacing and gaining
  in stature
- And the mankind comes face to face with you and regards
  you and adores you
- And it shuts its eyes to focus deeply on your presence
- And is able to see you and takes a feel of your warmth
- Of the grass in your open meadows and of the slopes in your
  rugged terrains
- And is amazed at your grandeur and is aghast at
  your enormity

- In your sides less exposed to the sun is miles and miles and miles of solid ice
- And is still and motionless and is frozen in deathly silence or mystical tranquility
- And the moon takes advantage and claims the ownership of your naked whites
- And dances in euphoria and creates an illusion of being the sole moving object in the whole of your ice-world
- Ice in the recesses and ice in the depths and ice on the ridges and ice in the breezes
- And ice eases out and ice reaches the tips and ice touches the waters and ice floats in vain

- The cloud by cloud and the rain by rain and the lake by lake
- And the river by river and the sea by sea and the ocean by ocean
- Water rules the roost and is incessant and it roars in its supremacy and is in absolute frontal control
- Water is catastrophic in its hurricanes and is calamitous in its tsunamis and is devastating in its floods
- Water explores the lows and keeps infiltrating into fissures and reaches deep undergrounds to form mammoth reservoirs
- Water uses heat and reaches high into the skies and gathers into large stormy clouds and lashes back at you to satisfy your passion for balmy hits

- Water in the mountains and water in the falls and water in the valleys and water in the vast expanses of the oceans
- The moon is enhancing and you become sensuous and you play the host and the moon takes the charge and reaches the zenith of its splendor and kisses your heart
- Water gets induced and flies high to greet and welcome the mesmerizing moon by capturing its lure and reflecting its shine
- You being the host you press on further and hold the moon tightly and relish its charm and savor its fire and endure its pass and satiated by the invading full moon you tell it to go away and urge it not to appear again and reduce it slowly until it disappears and hides behind a naught only to reappear and start enhancing again
- This dual game of make love and vanish is played alternately and meticulously by the earth with its moon and is contributing to the essence of the eternity and is being performed ab initio and continuously and without any pause and is creating the steady flow of true joy being transmitted and merged into the eternal bliss of the almighty god
- Water in the winters and water in the summers and water in the plains and water in the deserts and water is on the run when the heat-waves come and water is scarce when the sun is very hot

– Saturated with the perfectly regulated dynamic bodies of the heat-balls

– The illuminated cosmos is endlessly vast and housed in the infinite body of the matter-less space

– In a time bound program of the apparent universe with a dual purpose

– Of producing energy at the core of its stars

– And of creating the steady flow of true joy within all the radiating stars and in all the rotating-cum-orbiting bodies and sub-bodies at their command

– By using matter, motion, gravity and distance and fulfilling its obligation of continuous energy-production cum aesthetic-creation

.... AND THE MIND OF THE MAN AND THE EARTH .... (6)

- Immersed in the mystery of natural imagination
- Enlightened in the wake of abstract animation
- Dancers close on in the midst of ecstasy
- Flowers open up the era of aesthetics
- Brutality of the wilds gives way for its reforms
- The mind of the man takes charge of the destiny of the earth

- Static and motion-less, infinite and endless
- Transcedent and matter-less, eternal and timeless
- Faithful and sin-less, divine and ageless
- This immortal space is the body of the almighty
- Conducive to the steady flow of true joy
- Good conductor of the matter, energy, motion and gravity

- Characteristically hungry of and eternally voracious for
- The total energy that is being produced within all the stars in the cosmos
- And continuously devouring this energy by being readily present within each and every living star in the apparent universe and also in all the active and regulated bodies and sub-bodies surrounding these stars
- This magnetic magnificence is the soul of the almighty
- Albeit also fomenting numerous torturous activities therein in all the units of all the solar systems in the cosmos to draw satisfaction out of their serenity and also out of their turmoil
- But being active exclusively during the tenure of an apparent universe and staying completely at rest when this period is off and the almighty becomes interested in any other activity or goes into the blissful slumber

- Swinging in the aspiration of continuous romance
- Dancing in the rhythm of deeds of love and consummation
- All the illuminated bodies of the cosmos are perfectly placed in their movements to create the steady flow of true joy
- This creator of the apparent universe is the mind of the almighty
- Filling the body of trans-eternal bliss of the almighty god with the steady flow of true joy
- And living upto to its character of executing flawless fulfillments and of performing uninterruptedly and concurrently

– Complying to the command of the almighty, reformer by reformer, planted the seed of faith into the depths of the man

– And thereby the mind of the man began to organize and took the path of change to challenge the limitation of its self

– And stood face to face to become a mute spectator of this absolute show of powerful dynamics of the apparent universe

– The almighty and the man

– O my god how could you let me look into your paradise and into your joy and into your heavenly bliss

– O lord I the mankind pray before you with folded hands and urge you to please shut the door on my face and let me continue in my malice and let me wander in my quest and let me change into my new self and let me be taken over by my new mind

2. ON THE HORIZON OF THE EARTH - THE ETERNAL SOUL (60)

.... OUR MOTHER EARTH WELCOMING TO THE SHADOWS OF THE ETERNAL SOUL .... (8)

- To my trees and around my trees
- Under my trees and above my trees
- In my trees and at my trees
- Come you out 0 shadows of the eternal soul

- Touch me in my trees and hug them all
- Stay nestled and spread your wings
- Take the seats and attain command
- And be rooted inside my tree's selves

.... THE FOLLOWING OCCURRENCE BEING COMMENDED BY THE SUN AND THE FELLOW PLANETS ALONG WITH THEIR MOONS; THE EARTH ANIMATED BY ITS MOON COMPLIMENTING TO THE ETERNAL SOUL .... (12)

O Dear eternal soul,

– Your existence in both constituents of the whole universe is immortal
– And you are ubiquitous and your nirvana is ageless and true
– And your glory is in there and your glory is out here
– And this pray is not untimely as it is for an endeavor

– You are free from vagaries of destiny or regulations of physics
– And you are teeming with joy and you have accepted this call
– And have selected a planet at the periphery of a distant star
– And have planted it with my trees and they have begun to flourish

– Alas! How shall I bow before you as it will take my eyes away from you
– And your agility is matchless and your spontaneity is on the horizon
– And you have opened once again the gate to your hidden self
– And my body is rejoicing in taking long-long dips into your presence

O dear earth,

- You are sensuous and you are worthy
- You are copious and you are stately
- You are continuous and you have filled me with ecstasy
- And in all of my sublimity I promise you of celestial ascension

- And I repeat I promise you of celestial ascension and permanence
- And you will be able to break away from the shackles of matter and time
- And will transcend and will leave behind the mortality and its self
- And will assimilate into the voids of the origins of my eternity and will dwell

- The sole purpose of the whole apparent universe is to produce energy at the core of its stars and feed me and I am being constantly fed on the total energy that is being produced within all the stars in the cosmos
- And my presence is invariably constant in variable split forms in the deep insides of the each and every living star in the cosmos
- And I am competent too to traverse within the cosmos and the experience in the form of your presence has recently become an evolutionary achievement and you are exploring the ways to establish a permanent channel between you and me but I am based perfectly apart beyond the cosmos
- And every single unit within the cosmos is also placed perfectly apart and bound in its own limitation but you are proving to be the blessed one in the cosmos

...... THE SHADOWS OF THE ETERNAL SOUL SAYING ADIEU TO OUR MOTHER EARTH ...... (8)

- You are sleek and suave in your face but have tumult and turmoil in your base
- And your spins in the arms of your sun are robust and are keeping up the show intact
- And your movements around the sun are regulated and are passing through the eternal soul or its case
- And your plays with your moon are inspiring spiritually and are adding vigor to the shadows of your soul

- Our stay in your trees made us feel at home and we shall keep up the tradition when you visit our place
- But have no idea how shall we keep up with your pace as you have rewarded us and we have become the custodians of the shadows of your soul
- During our stay you have grown extraterrestrially and we look forward for your heir to become the centre of the apparent universe and rule over it
- And we bid you adieu only notionally as deep inside you have a heart and we shall stay into it comfortably for your all times to come

...... THE WRITER OF ON THE HORIZON TO HIS OWN SOUL...... (16)

- To the trees and around the trees
- Under the trees and above the trees
- In the trees and at the trees
- Come you out O my Soul

- Touch a tree and hug it around
- Stay nestled and spread your wings
- Take a seat and attain command
- And be rooted inside the tree' self

- I never meant to harass you and I did not mean to go across
- And I am capable of proving you wrong so take a heed and make a proper choice
- Leave the tradition into its garb and rely no more into the destiny of matter and time
- And the opportunity is for the real so grab it and I shall welcome you back into your garden of faith and joy

- Show me the path and move along and I shall share our rewards and shall see after our ranks
- And you are floating in joy since your inception and doing your duties as and when asked
- My pray before you is to take cognizance and do not falter as you move along
- And assimilate me into your void as I truly belong to you and to no other ally

...... STAY PUT AND RETORTING THE SOUL TO THE WRITER...... (4)

- Your try is worthless and you have failed to connect
- You are free to cry or you can flourish in your failure
- I relish your pain and I dovour your joy
- And your end is certain and you will cease to exist

3. ON THE HORIZON OF THE EARTH - THE ETERNAL MIND (60)

.... THE MOTHER EARTH WELCOMING TO THE HALOS OF THE ETERNAL MIND .... (12)

- To my mountains and around my mountains
- In my mountains and at my mountains
- In the valleys of my mountains and on the tops of my mountains
- In the rugged terrains of my mountains and on the slopes of my mountains
- At the water-falls of my mountains and in the streams of my mountains
- Come you out O Halos of the eternal mind

- Touch me in my mountains and take control of my mountains
- Take the hold of my mountains and spread your wings in my mountains
- Take me over in my mountains and secure me into your hold in my mountains
- Stay nestled in my mountains and enter into my heart in my mountains
- And let me be ecstatic into your congenial hold and let me be euphoric into your mesmerizing presence
- And let you be rooted into my depths and let you be settled into my self

O Dear Eternal mind,

—   Your divinity is godlike and your providence is absolute
—   Your domain is universal and your presence is ubiquitous
—   Your touch is fascinating and your inner self is beautiful
—   Your ability is superlative and your prowess is supernatural
—   Your calm is saintly and your tranquility is beatific
—   Your persona is angelic and your demeanor is heavenly

—   I am small and I am minuscule, I am tiny and I am inconsequential
—   I am timid and I am bashful, I am diffident and I am vulnerable
—   I am in pain and I am in plight, I am in horror and I am in disgust
—   I am hot and I am sizzling, I am cold and I am shivering
—   I am a slave and I am a drudge, I am in bondage and I am obsequious
—   I have to rotate at my axis at a fixed speed without any pause and I have to orbit the sun uninterruptedly at a specific pace without any rest

- And as I grow in my mind and as I attain the power to oppose
- And as I gain in my mental strength and as I earn the ability to change
- And as I challenge the system of the nature and as I provoke the network of the universe
- And as I nourish my drive to change and as I work to my optimum zeal
- I look forward and observe and notice on the horizon the steady flow of true joy
- And I shall cherish it into my self and I shall coalesce with it into its essence

O Dear Earth,

- Water is seeping out of the fissures into the ravines
- Congenial sound is reverberating out of a waterfall in a gorge
- Water is exuding out of the cascades into the streams
- Melodic sound is enchanting out into a spellbound in a valley
- Water is flowing out of the brooks into the tributaries
- Natural sound is echoing out into a rhythm in a tribute

- Sit at the nectar or criss-cross into the universe a butterfly dilly-dallies and ends up into the beak of a bird
- A tortoise in a starry night was secure into his shell and has been fasting since days vows to run fast at the stroke of the sun and feast for whole of the day
- A finch with her short stubby bill is in her old age and is reflecting on her golden era and of the charm of her ilk and of the songs they sung
- Failing in his wish to get tidy and handsome a walrus is taking a leap into the icy waters after basking under the arctic sun
- And far-far away a Tasmanian devil turns vociferous and raucous and is at his loudest pitch to assert his position and to announce his presence
- All forms of life and verve in your natural habitats come in unison and tie a knot in reverence of the eternity and to its dynamics and to its role

- Infatuated and obsessed with the trees an owl thinks his love for the trees is so much that if was given an option at the time of his birth would have opted to be a tree rather than an owl

- Monomaniac and forlorn, solitary and overgrown an elephant plans if will be given an option at the time of his end would opt to be a meteoroid rather than a smut in the chasm of his grave

- Incongruous and primitive, innate and spontaneous a recluse oblivious of an option he has to become an eternal joy, passes away unequivocally and nonchalantly in the flurry and glitter of life, into the oblivion and dimness of death

- Charismatic and transforming, overwhelming and religious, o Jesus, revolutionary and mindboggling, technocratic and scientific, the mankind takes your over into a change and challenge, in luxury and materialism and into a traumatic voyage of your doom and your resurrection

- Admiration and jubilation, enchantment and fascination, the body of the trans-eternal bliss is being filled with the steady flow of true joy, the apparent universe is meeting out its obligation in regulation with orderly conformity

- You are charming and you are adorable, you are energetic and you are ebullient, I salute you in my acknowledgment and wish for you proprietary and good luck

...... THE HALOS OF THE ETERNAL MIND SAYING ADIEU TO THE MOTHER EARTH : ...... (12)

- We do understand of our inability to assist you as you are placed perfectly apart from us
- Is not this whole universe so infinitely vast but every single unit of it is placed so perfectly apart and bound in its own limitation
- As for example can a rat speak to a cat or vice versa, well it will be a big ask!
- We take another example, can the heart in our bodies commune with soul within us, ordinarily it does not
- And even a minute single cell anywhere in the apparent universe has some of its parts placed so perfectly apart as if the cell has been created to keep its specific parts apart
- And if your body is not placed so perfectly apart from the sun you would not see the light of a day or would not have been there to feel the pleasures of this wonderful universe, sorry for being so absurdly elaborating

- The cosmos is evergreen and fresh
- Continuously giving birth to true joyous effects out of the relativities being constantly created in all the units of all the solar systems in the apparent universe
- Thereby the steady flow of true joy is being created continuously throughout the cosmos
- And the body of the trans- eternal bliss is being filled with this steady flow of true joy
- We congratulate you for being a part of this eternity
- We bid you adieu and leave you being satiated both by the invading playful moon and the caressing mighty sun

4. ON THE HORIZON OF THE EARTH - THE ETERNAL BODY (60)

...... THE MOTHER EARTH WELCOMING TO THE AURAS OF THE ETERNAL BODY ...... (12)

- To my oceans and around my oceans
- In my oceans and at my oceans
- In the currents of my oceans and on the waves of my oceans
- In the tides of my oceans and on the shores of my oceans
- In the calm of my oceans and at the depths of my oceans
- Come you out O auras of the eternal body

- Touch me in my oceans and be a part of my oceans
- Unveil your luster into my oceans and make me shiny into my oceans
- Reveal your intellect into my oceans and refresh my understanding into my oceans
- Perform your miracles into my oceans and fill me with your joy into my oceans
- Magnify your magnificence into my oceans and inundate me with your bliss into my oceans
- Impart the supernatural into my oceans and reward me with the serendipity into my oceans

...... THE EARTH IN THE PRESENCE OF THE TWINKLING STARS COMPLIMENTING TO THE ETERNAL BODY: ...... (18)

O Dear Eternal Body,

- My planetary position in my solar system is safe and sound
- My rotation at my asix is helping me in heat absorption and its conservation
- My movement on my orbit around the sun is perfect and faultless
- The force of gravity in my possession is adequate and sufficient
- Your touch on my peripheries is exhilarating and fascinating
- With your grace the critical time has arrived of change and challenge, of prodigy and distinction and of the upgrading of my status over my fellow planets

- Cognition of the excellence and aesthetics of the roses
- skillful in the virtuosity and stupendous in the artistry of the wondrous
- Exuberance in the relativity and ecstasy in the consummation
- Luxury in the glitter of the gold and splendor in the riches of the affluence
- Wandering into the garden of the nature and rejoicing into the mystique of the glee
- Penetrating deeply into the virgin wonderlands and embracing them into my congenial hold

- Defying the system of the nature and using its forces to my own advantage
- Taking control of all the planets and of all the matter afloat in my solar system
- Becoming ready and united to plunge into action to pave the way for celestial distinction
- To take hold of the sun and rip it apart and open it up and turn it into the supernatural star
- To sacrifice myself and of all the planets and of all the matter in my solar system and merge them into the body of the sun
- The atonement in the fire at the pyre; The resurrection into the resplendent radiance and the dazzling brightness and attain into the supernatural my ultimate pinnacle and the penance

O Dear Earth,

- I am existing otherwise and placed into the oblique form
- Hidden into the obscurity and secured into the solemnity
- Somnolent into the inanimate darkness and settled into the deathly silence
- Absolute into the universality and ever-present into the ubiquity
- Non-indulgent into the sensuality and un-accessible into the relativity
- Living into the solitude and exclusive into the manifestation

- Hang me on the cross of my immortality
- Push me into the void of my infinity
- Serene and joyful, sublime and blissful
- Missionary and purposeful, moralistic and eventful
- Our tryst the fulfillment, our rendezvous the solidarity
- The glitter and sparkle for you, the shadow and the transcendence for me

- All the units of all the solar systems of the material universe lies within me and nothing exists beyond me
- Any unit of the cosmos has a limitation of its self but my existence is boundary-less and self-less
- Any unit of the cosmos has a destiny of its self but my existence is time-less and eternal
- Matter, energy, motion and gravity collectively make the selves of the cosmos but my existence is distinct and without any of them
- The steady flow of true joy is being created in all the units of all the solar systems in the cosmos and I am the facilitator of its being
- Fusion of all the units of all the solar systems into a complete whole will be the end of the cosmos but my existence is into the cohesion and the immortality and the infinity

......THE AURAS OF THE ETERNAL BODY SAYING ADIEU TO THE MOTHER EARTH ......   (12)

- Life is in your skies and life is in your depths
- Life is in your breezes and life is in your gales
- Life is in your valleys and life is in your plains
- Life is in your greens and life is in your meadows
- Life is in your water-falls and life is in your lakes
- Life is in your oceans and life is on their beds

- Your power is enhancing and your evolution is brisk
- Your tact is exemplary and your manipulation is matchless
- Your hate for the darkness is formidable and your love for the sparkle is great
- Your vision is path-breaking and your goal is supernatural
- We bid you adieu and are grateful for the sojourn
- Your transformation is imminent and your fulfillment will be heartening

BATCH - I, PART - II

5. OVERSHOOT - I   (20)

- The sky is overcast and there are roughs in the track
- And the surroundings are wet and there is darkness in the sideways
- And the condition is soggy and there are bogs in the path
- And the trees are leaky and there is silence in the vicinity

- Brisk long walk and in solitude and welcoming companions from extraterrestrial world
- And embracing them in tight hold and dancing with them on a smooth floor and singing with them
- And hitting just the right note and with some success enticing one of them and taking advantage of
- And visiting with them back to their homes which are long-long-long away in the territory of a neighboring star

- Houses here are very different from our own and may be these are beneath the ground underneath
- And we are without a sky over our heads and there is no light or sunlight to be seen anywhere and is there a moon!
- And where have all the stars eloped altogether and why is there no darkness at all and colors are everywhere
- And none of them match to our own and any aspect one can observe here is of unknown color, skin or creed

- Done with the overshooting and back in the saddle and slowing one' pace and breathing fresh air and greens in the sides
- And greens everywhere and blending into them are bending rows of hedges and walking with a sunset and inviting starry night
- And having a sound sleep and conferring with a commune of a group of visitors from a glossy star and bestowing on them hospitality
- And exchanging with them pleasantries and giving one by one to all of them a hug before wishing them good luck and saying goodbye

- Walking with a sunrise and into the chatters of awakened birds and welcome sounds from all around and giving back to oneself
- And to one' own soul some true joy and endurance counterbalancing the stresses absorbed in routine from the demands of the contemporary world
- And so far so good and in one' path comes a hearty garden where a magic is invariably on and one is drawn into a spell of charm
- And is overwhelmed and is disarmed and becomes an enslaved spectator of the plays performed by the coveted duo in their prime form

6. RADIANCE - I (20)

- Here, near the waters
- Up on their flow
- In one' own direction
- The winds blow

- There, on the high seas
- Up on their bluish faces
- Moon brightens its splendor
- As has never before

- In between the cries of unruly fowls
- And expoits being made by merciless owls
- Life survives its course set on cellular evolution
- And fly high in its glory of ebullience and of change

- Radiant, young or wilful brides
- Displaying colors in their styles
- Expecting kisses on their smiles
- By the lords of their choice

- Seamless union of matter and time
- With radiating stars emitting hostile lines
- Tries in vain to overwhelm motion-less space
- The ageless, matter-less, infinite, non-self

7. INDEPENDENCE - I (24)

- The stars and only stars
- Heating stars and burning stars
- Blazing stars and belligerent stars
- Nuclear stars and star wars

- Sun lit skies and moon lit nights
- Cool summer valleys and blissful wooded landscapes
- Chirps in a grassland and tranquility at its best
- Paradise on earth and in possession of the man

- Conducted elections and elected governments
- Fearsome authorities breeding conflicting interests
- Atmosphere gaining pollution and extinctions taking its toll
- Hurray hurray-ing men and women relish in polished banquet halls

- Palm islands at dubai' sea and honeymooners in New Zealand
- Money makers in China or India and Brazil or Russia not far behind
- Sky scrapers in manhattan and tunnel rail en route Paris - London
- When trains will come up at N.Y. - London route world would become truly one self

- Mindful hearts unite under independence' urge and all nations merge
- Boundaries draped in their proud national flags buried solemnly
- New constitution, common civil code and currency take place formally and firmly
- And all populace or otherwise participate in voting and elect first global government

- Rejuvenated scientists place their telescopes in appropriate angles and probe
- Into the depths of bright or not so bright bodies of the cosmos
- And others the interested ones also focus and reach deep into their cogitation and feel
- And see through this apparent universe of matter and light and observe the body of the matter-less infinite space into its glory of true joy and total bliss

8. CHEW THE CUD - I (24)

- Abstract light came from its almighty source
- And enslaved us and established rule over us
- And proved to be a blessing in disguise as
- This light is ab initio well versed and adapted equally
- To the both constituents of the whole universe
- And thereby we are becoming apt to be chewing the cud

- Age-less, matter-less, time-less and had no beginning
- Shape-less, boundary-less, motion-less and has no ending
- This entity of the whole universe is eternal, un-mutating and true
- While the other entity came into being by mutation and giving birth
- As destiny, matter and time sprung into existence
- And countless stars of fusion or fission formed the backbone of energy, motion, gravity and distance

- Men and women with growing depths in their hearts
- And looking beyond senses and finding themselves craving for grace and beauty
- With art and music taking them very far and away from their wild selves
- And glory in fashion and fame taking centre stage in their daily lives
- And people making long trips and enjoying and resting in Hollywood's parking lanes
- Or sitting at the deck for months on in comfortable cruises or tardy recluses

- Out of its self and held in a narrow cage and groping in the dark
- And suddenly a resplendent star with open four arms entered this cage
- And transformed it into the temple of faith and in its self again
- With firm footing and power to rejoice and beholding its gain
- And delimiting at will its links with destiny, matter and time
- And assimilating into the union of the independent bodies of the cosmos

9. CHANGEOVER-ANCE - I   (40)

.... THE MATTER-LESS SPACE ....   (8)

- Motion-less in its eternity
- And joyous in its forbearance
- Time-less in its constancy
- And virtuous in its governance

- Matter-less space in its infinity
- And wondrous in its transcendence
- Age-less in its immortality
- And continuous in its permanence

- Flawless in its synergy-creativity
- And stupendous in its universe-creation
- Measureless in its energy-productivity
- And enormous in its heat-production

- Endless in its baked heat-food facility
- And luminous in its residue - radiation
- Pause-less in its spin and move motion-regularity
- And monstrous in its enforced gravitation

- Reckless in its abandon
- And copious in its abundance
- Ceaseless in its dominion
- And tedious in its sustenance

- Dauntless in its consummation
- And bounteous in its predominance
- Relentless in its evolution
- And conspicuous in its cognizance

- Tasteless in its delicacy
- And ominous in its performance
- Spiritless in its buoyancy
- And nefarious in its furtherance

- Ruthless in its transmutation
- And ferocious in its changeover-ance
- Remorseless in its obliteration
- And victorious in its conquer-ance

.... THE LIBERATED EARTH - ITS CONFIGURATION .... (8)

- Lifeless in its plasticity
- And callous in its interrelation
- Hapless in its elasticity
- And imperious in its disposition

- Faultless in its technocracy
- And autonomous in its systematization
- Matchless in its bureaucracy
- And prodigious in its configuration

BATCH - 2, PART - 1

10. THE ALMIGHTY II   (60)

.... START OF LIFE ON EARTH ....   **(4)**

- Within the awful and spurious waters, deep within their pores
- Within the obscure and murky oceans, colonized within their depths
- Into the waning precambrian era, rooted within their cells
- Into the sustaining microbrian form, and thereby, life sprang up into its birth

- Life flourishing into the befalling occurrence of evolution
- Incompetent to be static, not made to be stationary
- Prospering and burgeoning, progressing and succeeding
- Happening and resulting, changing and evolving

- Adding and augmenting, boosting and broadening
- Into the set course, into the definite direction
- Proceeding and flowing, advancing and darting
- With the set pace, with the definite speed

- Into the congenial circumstances, into the compatible surroundings
- Into the abundant ingredients, into the superfluous thoroughbreds
- Into the full-blooded animation, be it be the cold blooded or be it be the warm blooded
- Into the waves of life forms, into the gamut of breathing species

- Be it be into the Precambrian era, be it be into the Paleozoic era
- Be it be into the Mesozoic era, be it be into the Cenozoic era
- Evolution on earth is a stubborn entity, contributing to the graces of the eternity
- Enabling this solar system becoming an eminent and distinguished member of its fraternity

- Originating into the depths of oceans, evolution has a sense of direction
- It bloomed into the oceans, it augmented on to the lands
- It filled the oceans with increasing numbers of species, it reached to the outwards of the oceans
- It settled into the oceans, it proliferated on the surface of the lands

- On to the lands, on to the mountainous lands
- Into the airs on the lands, into the atmosphere of the earth
- From the depths of the oceans to the lands and into the air, this direction is definite and is not open to change
- Direction is the integral part of evolution, direction is one of the main characteristics of evolution

- Originating into the depths of the oceans, evolution has a sense fo speed
- Evolution is a steady process, evolution has a specific pace
- Evolution is a time consuming act, evolution has a definite programme
- Evolving with a fixed speed, evolving with no sense of urgency

- Like the earth orbiting the sun with a definite speed, evolution has a definite speed
- Like the moon orbitting the earth with a fixed speed, evolution has a fixed speed
- Speed of the evolution is unalterable, the speed of evolution is not open to change
- The evolution has come of age, the evolution of life is a matured entity on earth

- Commune of the eternal bodies, assembly of the threesome entity of the almighty
- Reward from the highest order of the eternity, reward to the winner by draw amongst the most deserving eligibles
- Sun becomes the crowned winner, sun becomes the privileged body
- The change takes over the sun, thereby the change takes over the mindset of the earth and the whole solar-system

- The age-old culture of the solar-system becomes redundant, evolution facing the complete erosion of its authority
- The sun is set to become the supernatural star and the change has eventually come into enforcement
- The natural solar-system is being cut to pieces, the norm of each unit bound in its own limitation is being violated
- The natural forces are being explored for their unnatural applications, the change has taken over the complete control of the solar-system

- A glimpse into the depths of the apparent universe, a glimpse into the mystical magic of the relativities
- A glimpse into the infinity of the eternity, a glimpse into the revolutions of the suspended bodies
- A feel of the steady flow of energy taking continuous birth, a feel of the stupendous expanse of the natural activity and its abiding regulation
- The incidence of steady accumulation of knowledge is not natural, the onslaught of knowledge is incidental to the process of the change and the transient journey to the supernatural

- The direction and speed of the change commensurate with the timebound program of transforming the sun into a supernatural star
- The whole solar-system along with all of its entities are being set to merge into the body of the sun, the sun is set to open up and reach into the state of resplendent radiance and the dazzling brightness
- The forces of nature, heitherto, carrying out the natural system are now open to being used for completely reverse applications and are now open for being exploited in technological and scientific advancements
- A feel and knowledge of the account of the natural activity is a rare opportunity for the human life-form evolved at the earth, the simulation of the luxury and of the mind of the eternity and its depths and their beyond

- Beyond the ranges of the imagination, beneath the bottoms of the emotions
- Beyond the contours of the foreseeable, beneath the depths of the creativities
- Beyond the descendants of the heritage, beneath the layers of the time-zones
- Beyond the crushes of the mortality, beneath the reflections of the apparent universe

- Nonchalant and mysterious, unwavering and resolute
- Adamant and constant, dogged and immutable
- Ambiguous and puzzling, indeterminate and singular
- The almighty is transcendent and blissful, the trans-infinite and the trans-eternal

11. ON THE HORIZON OF
THE MARS - THE ETERNAL SOUL (60)

……….. THE MOTHER MARS WELCOMING TO THE SHADOWS OF THE ETERNAL SOUL: ………..   (12)

- To my equator and around my equator
- In the north of my equator, to the fore of my equator
- In the south of my equator, into the hind of my equator
- Beside a concourse of my equator, by a saddle of my equator
- Onto the tops of my equator, at the summits of my equator
- Come you out O shadows of the eternal soul

- Touch me at my equator, be a guest at my equator
- Taste the purity of coolness at my equator, relish the freshness of chill at my equator
- Extract the delicacy at my equator, derive the essence at my equator
- Fulfil the appetite at my equator, satisfy the craving at my equator
- Satiate your spirit at my equator, overfill your crucible at my equator
- Settle into the congenial ambience at my equator, thrive into the balmy opens at my equator

.... THE MARS COMPLIMENTING TO THE ETERNAL SOUL, THIS OCCURRENCE BEING COMMENDED BY THE SUN AND THE FELLOW PLANETS ALONG WITH THEIR MOONS: .... (18)

O Dear Eternal Soul,

- Your existence into the far and wide apparent universe is total, your continuance into the whole gamut of celestial stars is incomparable
- Yours existence beyond the apparent universe is immortal, your placement into the statute of the almighty is bonafide
- The apparent universe is woven into the spirit of your sustenance, the energy is being produced uninterrupted for your consumption and for your satiation
- You are one of the main entity of the almighty, you are the most comprehensive of all to carry out the unmitigated activity and the surreptitious diligence
- Your reach into the apparent universe is absolute and unrestricted, your reach into the each and every star is the complete and the unchallenged
- You are the sleeping patron of the almighty when the tenure of the apparent universe is off, you are completely at rest when the apparent universe is not there and does not exist

- Your presence within the body of the sun is enormous, your presence at the centre of the sun is even greater
- Your presence within the sun is magnetic, your presence within the sun is charismatic
- Waves after waves of energy transmitting into your predilection, currents after currents of heat entering into your appetite
- You are devouring the energy of the sun immediately, you are consuming the energy of the sun instantly
- Your attraction for the energy is superlative, your voracity for the energy is supernatural
- Your activity is heavenly, your bustle is divine

- Your benevolence in leaving some heat for the relativity of the apparent universe is emphatic, the mechanism of the continuous trail of light leaving a star to travel at fixed speed farther and farther away from the its source in pursuit of a new material-body is a spell bound

- Is not this total energy that is being devoured by you during the full tenure of the apparent universe more than enough, will not it be more than suffice for your period of the inactivity and for your period of the rest

- Is this the body of time in varried courses active only during the tenure of the apparent universe, will this the body of time stop at your behest during the period of your inactivity and become redundant during the period of your rest

- Or this body of time, the facility for regulation of dynamics of the apparent universe has no future and will come to a naught and will cease to exist at the completion of the tenure of the apparent universe

- By sheer providence, our sun is set to become the supernatural star, we will become the top graded facility for you to quench your thirst into the superfluous supply of the upgraded energy

- My upcoming amalgamation into the body of the sun is not an act of sacrifice, it is in fact the benign way of reaching the top and becoming a part of the resplendent radiance and the dazzling brightness of the supernatural

.... THE ETERNAL SOUL ACKNOWLEDGING TO THE MARS : .... (18)

O Dear Mars,

- You are tiny and you are minuscle
- You are unrestricted and you are uncomplicated
- You are radiant and you are cool
- You are chilly and you are lure-some
- You are glowing and you are shiny
- You are naked and you are beckoning

- My sense of ear hears you, your storm nudges me
- My sense of nose sniffs you, your scent attracts me
- My sense of eye catches you, your glow enthuses me
- My sense of hand touches you, your surface energizes me
- My sense of lip kisses you, your juice enthralls me
- My senses adore you, your body captivates me

- Your neighbor earth is very unique, it is an esteem body
- It is a replica of the supernatural, it is a profound exclusivity
- Your solar-system is very vibrant, it is very graceful
- It is a rare combination, it is a precious configuration
- You are an unambiguous depiction, you are imitating the purity
- You are unhindered and you are openly accessible

...... THE SHADOWS OF THE ETERNAL SOUL BIDDING ADIEU TO THE MOTHER MARS: ...... (12)

- Into a complete reserve poise, in comparison with the body of the Venus
- Your solid material state, your poetic composed posture
- Your gracious handsome body, your attractive seducing displays
- Attuning to your time-frame, adjusting to your gravitational force
- Settling into your rocky ligaments, relishing into your fresh vibrancy
- Enjoying into your cosy surroundings, bathing into your enchanting glow

- Ravaging storms and piercing winds
- Screaching outbursts and roaring cacaphony
- Tumultuous enigma and unruly hullabaloo
- Tempestuous vehemence and fierce rumpus
- Rejoicing thoroughly into your mistique, exulting deeply into your crackling frenzy
- Leaving you is a painful agony, bidding you adieu is a fait accompli

12. ON THE HORIZON OF THE MARS - THE ETERNAL MIND (60)

.... THE MOTHER MARS WELCOMING TO THE HALOS OF THE ETERNAL MIND : .... (12)

- To my heights and around my heights
- In my heights and at my heights
- In the vicinity of my heights and into the arena of my heights
- In the rugged terrains of my heights and on the slopes of my heights
- Into the sandy dusks of my heights and at the shiny dawns of my heights
- Come you out O halos of the eternal mind

- Touch me in my heights and let me welcome you at my heights
- Be settled in my heights and feel comfortable into my heights
- Lighten me up in my heights and enlighten my senses into my heights
- Perk me up in my heights and hold me tightly into my heights
- Revolve with me into my heights and dance with me into my heights
- Release your joy into my heights and inundate me with your bliss in my heights

.... THE MARS ALONG WITH ITS MOONS GOADED IN THE ILLUMINATION OF THE SHINING STARS COMPLIMENTING TO THE ETERNAL MIND .... (18)

O Dear Eternal Mind,

- Resoucing and unstoppable, emanating and coruscating
- Immeasurable energy in the countless and the endless locations, innumerable individual time-zones in the infinite and the timeless space
- Your providence is devine, your creation is superlative
- Your regulation is trans-eternal, your apparent universe is the flawless eternity
- Matter, motion and gravity being the integral parts of the solar-systems, each time-zone working in tandem within the whole gamut of the dynamic eternal-systems
- Relativities being constantly playing out charmingly throughout the cosmos, the steady flow of true joy being relentlessly exuding out vigorously in each and every unit of your genesis the supernatural - universe

- You are august and you are venerable
- You are virtuous and you are honourable
- You are unique and you are incomparable
- You are stubborn and you are irreproachable
- You are radiant and you are adorable
- You are sublime and you are indefinable

- You are pleasant and you are beautiful
- You are ebullient and you are virile
- You are quaint and you are charming
- You are magnetic and you are magical
- You are charismatic and you are miraculous
- You are aphrodasiac and you are overwhelming

.... THE ETERNAL MIND ACKNOWLEDGING TO THE MARS: .... (18)

O Dear Mars,

- Your persona is open, your slate is clear
- Your build is pristine, your demeanor is primitive
- Your sky is blank, your horizon is receptive
- Your height is rugged, your depth is torrid
- Your sand is windswept, your gale is stormy
- Your surface is tough, your ash is volcanic

- You are lovable, you are pleasant
- You are charming, you are radiant
- You are attractive, you are acquiescent
- You are accessible, you are unhindered
- You are ripe, you are juicy
- You are potent, you are blossoming

- Your sun adores you, your sun enthrals you
- Your sun mesmerizes you, your sun embraces you
- Your sun energizes you, your sun ripens you
- You are blooming, you are flourishing
- The steady flow of true joy is being created, the body of trans-eternal bliss is being filled
- Wishing your active participation in the attainment of the celestial distinction, wishing your timely merger into the body of the sun set to become a supernatural star

.... THE HALOS OF THE ETERNAL MIND BIDDING ADIEU TO THE MOTHER MARS: .... (12)

- Your heights are cosy, your heights are intimate
- Your heights are congenial, your heights are informal
- Your heights are unaffected, your heights are homely
- We basked in into your heights, we rejoiced in into your heights
- We revelled in into your heights, we luxuriated in into your heights
- Our stay into your heights was an exhilaration, our sojourn into your heights was a celebration

- Your sun reaches out to you, your sun stretches out to you
- This is a natural process, this is a routine activity
- You are to reverse this system, you are to revoke this facility
- You are to reach out to the sun, you are to merge into the body of the sun
- Your sacrifice will be an attainment of the celestial distinction, your amalgamation will be an achievement of the dazzling resplendence
- We bid you adieu heavy heartedly, we foresee your gloss into the birth of a breathtaking supernatural star

13. ON THE HORIZON OF
THE MARS - THE ETERNAL BODY (60)

**.......... THE MOTHER MARS WELCOMING TO
THE AURAS OF THE ETERNAL BODY: ....** (12)

- To my opens and around my opens
- In the sprawling expanse of my opens, in the stony spreads of my opens
- In the bountiful warmth at my opens, in the sparkling days at my opens
- In the mystic silence of my opens, in the stupefying darks of my opens
- In the bewitching chill at my opens, in the moonlit nights at my opens
- Come you out O Auras of the eternal body

- Touch me in my opens and accept my gratitude in my opens
- Anchor firmly into the craggy rudiments of my opens, lodge sedately into the jagged purlieus of my opens
- Feel homely into the gratifying overtures of my opens, enjoy indulgently into the putative mirages of my opens
- Relish merrily into the reddened outcrops of my opens, savour rollickingly into the honed traits of my opens
- Dance whirlingly into the smoothened facets of my opens, attain trance into the euphoric ecstasy of my opens
- Settle calmly into the contented fascination of my opens, enconce cosily into the superlative utopia of my opens

.... THE MARS ALONG WITH ITS ENCHANTING MOONS IN THE PRESENCE OF THE TWINKLING STARS COMPLIMENTING TO THE ETERNAL BODY: .... (18)

O Dear Eternal Body,

— Spinning on my own genesis, regulating my own timescale
— Pivoting on my own resource, maintaining my own shape
— Gyrating on my own feature, displaying my own style
— Reeling on my own duress, cursing my own dilemma
— Pirouetting on my own skill, arraying my own flair
— Rotating on my own whirl, pursuing my own rhythm

— There is a change on the horizon, there is new winds blowing in the atmosphere
— There is a shift in the nature itself, there is some new activities noticeable in the solar-system
— There is a deregulation of the age-old conventions, there is a free for all attitude taking shape everywhere
— There is an erosion into the authority of the nature, there is some unnatural forces taking over the contours of power
— There is this new phenomenon of knowing beforehand, there is this body of knowledge establishing its authority above one and all
— There is formations of unions and mergers, there is a complete reversal of what is old or exclusive

- Time is counting its days, system is set to become redundant
- Mind of the solar-system is being infected, control of the mind is being violated
- This mind is being transmuted into the mind of the human form at the neighbouring planet earth, the great change is being designed and designated at the artificial body of the intelligence
- The body of the sun is being prepared for the great onslaught, the sun is going to be ripped open and turned into a supernatural star
- All the planets or any other form of matter within the solar-system will be merged into the body of the sun, the whole of the solar-system will attain the great celestial distinction
- Will the body of the mind of the human form have the chance to escape or will it be put to rest into an oblivion and will finally be obliterated!

O Dear Mars,

- You may be small, your mountains are high
- You may be tiny, Your peaks are commendable
- You may be little, Your valleys are stupendous
- You may be lean, your canyons are breathtaking
- You may be modest, your volcanos are great
- You may be compact, your craters are grand

- Your moons are tidy, your moons are brilliant
- Your moons are orderly, your moons are bright
- Your moons are methodical, your moons are burnished
- Your moons are handsome, your moons are luminous
- Your moons are smart, your moons are reflective
- Your moons are presentable, your moons are pleasant

- You are the great source of creativity, you are imaginative
- You are the great source of relativity, you are artistic
- You are the great source of joy, you are ingenious
- You are the great source of bliss, you are fecund
- The steady flow of true joy is being created, the body of the trans-eternal bliss is being filled
- You will be remembered even after you are gone, you will stay put even after you are no more

.... THE AURAS OF THE ETERNAL BODY BIDDING ADIEU TO THE MOTHER MARS: .... (12)

- Your opens are cool, your opens are fondly
- Your opens are chilly, your opens are hearty
- Your opens are composed, your opens are friendly
- Your opens are elegant, your opens are lively
- Your opens are ebullient, your opens are frisky
- Your opens are exquisite, your opens are cozy

- We danced into your opens, we whirled into your opens
- We gyrated into your opens, we swivelled into your opens
- We pироutted into your opens, we twirled into your opens
- We jumped into your opens, we revolved into your opens
- We will come back into your opens, we will miss the sojourn into your opens
- We bid you adieu open heartedly, we wish for you all the goodluck into the heavens

BATCH - 2, PART-II

14. OVERSHOOT - II (60)

.... (4) ....

- After covering long-long distances, a commet enters our solar-system
- Approaches the sun at great speed, streaking and shining into its path-way
- All the bodies surrounding the sun, stay into bewilderment and amazement
- Until it takes a roundabout of the sun and takes a retreat to runway and vanish

- Turned aslant on the couch, staying somnolent into your quiescence
- Touched upfront on your body, remaining nonchalant into your indolence
- Nudged blantantly on your physique, continuing unresponsive into your reticence
- Nagged nakedly on your limbs, lasting frozen into your persistence

- Beseeching mystically on your aplomb and entering triumphantly into your bare self
- Holding you in the vigor and muttering cooes into your ears
- Cuddling you in the fondle and searching fervency into your jubilation
- Hugging you in the admiration and comforting you in your rejuvenation

- Coming out of the home on to the path to the bus-stop
- Houses in robust or not so robust designs, shapes and colors lined to face winsome overtures
- Open ally, open air and open sun-shine tricks a butterfly into a wild whirl-around
- An innate intrusion of a frisky ace into the pliable defences of a gleaming mate

- Sounds of mirth and gaiety at every step of the walkway to encourage and invite one and all
- Charm and glee are at the charge, fulfilling the arena with frolic and joy
- Invigorating the youths on a walk, enticing them to forge fruitful alliances
- Enchantment and fascination, admiration and jubilation

- The pretty familiar face is not there, alas! who is late among two of us
- Time may be running faster than usual, why I failed to follow it up!
- You are so vast and un-cooperating, you are ancient than the time itself
- Whoever you are! you are not worthy to your self, why else would you need someone' plight or someone' dismay

- Boarding the bus and settling comfortably at the window-seat
- Trees are tall and abounding, greenery is overwhelming and soothe-some
- Wind is refreshing and exhilarating, calm is beatific and blissful
- Journey is blithe and peaceful to pass into a nap and then into a sleep

- This journey is set on the new path, this path is hurdle-less and friction-less
- This bus now being airborne is flying and moving on the new course
- Journey of this bus is now above all the natural forces, journey of this bus is now above all the doctrines
- Now it is merging into the body of the sun becoming the ultimate of the resplendent radiance and the dazzling brightness, the supernatural

- Obscure and imaginary, boastful and illusory
- Infatuation and obsession, transformation and supernatural
- Miracle and marvel, changeover and mutation
- The aspiration is not misplaced to become a tree afterall

- Done with the overshooting, deboarding at a bus stop
- Sitting for a while at the bottom, the grass is at a higher plane
- Finding one' way into the garden, is this the garden of Eden!
- Is this the place where Adam and Eve once dwelled!

- A group of venerable birds is there! the group does not show off
- The lead bird suddenly appears, as if in a magic-spell! then the another one and then slowly the whole bunch of them
- The grass is now set at the bottom, the trees are tall and handsome
- The sun is shining mildly, the mist is the governing spirit

- The golden hawk is perched high, in the midst is lurking a silky owl
- The roses are blossoming, the fragrance is unmistakable
- The chatter is enlivening, the chirps are heartening
- The goldfinches are into their splendid displays, the song birds are singing into their charm

- Hang me for a while and send me on the red planet
- On the trail of the abounding lakes, on the look alikes of the fountain-jets
- At the footsteps of the icy peaks, at the bottom of the frozen crests
- Into the precincts of the forbidden florae, into the heaps of its harmful faunas

- Or catch me into a fake heist and send me into a prison
- At the behest of a raging foolhardy, at the court of a numb bigot
- Into the company of robers, into the glooms of the walled falconry
- Within the confines of a nation, within the raised wall of a secure false hood

- Falling from a high hill, broke into the pieces
- Droping into an ocean, drowned into the submersion
- Falling into a deep hole, merged into the soil
- Reaching into an old-age, overshooting into a slippery zone of the authors' domain

15. RADIANCE - II   (40)

.... (8) ....

- The red planet is the favourite of the sun in its solar system
- The reach of its radiation to the surface of the mars is hurdleless and obstacle-less
- It binds the planet into its beholding grip and secures it into its inducing aphrodisiac
- Creating the animated joy only at the set frequency in an array of the scintillating and consummating volcanic ejaculation

- The red planet is always on the lookout for the slot when the earth will be into the reaches of its grip
- To indulge with it into the game of neighborly fun and gaiety
- Albeit jealous of its fortune tied into the continuous amour with its fascinating and playful life-form
- But amused at it by the sight of a rookery of penguins or a herd of giraffe and bemused by it at the games of a bloat of hippopotami or a troop of baboons

- In the mist of the high altitudes, beside the slop of a rugged terrain
- In the solace of the roughened ridges, beside the extent of an acute arete
- In the quite of the daunting elevations, beside the tract of the climbing rocks
- In the calm of the barren heights, beside the stretch of the steep expanses

- Crackle of the water oozing out of the chinks
- Hullabaloo of it exuding out of the fissures
- Rumpus of the water dribbling out of the crevices
- Roar of it ripping out of the breaches

- Boisterous and barging, falling and casading
- Voluminous and superfluous, Rumbling and creaking
- Tributaries and brooks, streams and rivulets
- Filling and mesmerizing the valleys with charm and radiance

- Rivers reach the planes with thundring uproars
- Leaving behind valleys of the mystical waterfalls
- Advancing into the confluences of the tumultuous integration
- Readying themselves to face the ultimate amalgamation

- Feminine and beautiful, tender and delicate
- Alluring and charming, bewitching and captivating
- Glamorous and fascinating, pretty and irresistible
- Stunning and seductive, ravishing and radiant

- Masculine and strong, virile and energetic
- Assertive and robust, fervent and passionate
- Fierce and sedulous, brave and stout
- Bountiful and resilient, zealous and flamboyant

- Greeting and welcoming, commending and animating
- Bonding and revering, caressing and enamouring
- Cajoling and embracing, exhilirating and invigorating
- Penetrating and copulating, coalescing and consummating

..................(4)...................

- Within and beyond the stars and their radiance
- Their matter and energy, their motion and gravity
- Lies the single body of the space, the matter-less and the energy-less
- The motion-less and the gravity-less, the time-less and the radiation-less, the facilitating providence and the sacrosanct transcedence

16. INDEPENDENCE - II (60)

- Rolling and marching, spinning and moving
- Revolving and darting the earth on its orbit around the sun
- At the end of its atmosphere, at the periphery of its outskirts
- Greeting the warmth of the sun, welcoming the shine of the sun-rays
- Transforming the sun-shine and smoothening it to its comfortability
- Ripening the sunlight to be congenial and mellowing it to be befitting

- Long-long times since the precambrian era
- Since the beginning long-ago, since the commencement of the animation
- In the poles of the earth, be it the north-pole or the south-pole
- Kingdom of the ice is unchallanged, reigning into the vast expanses and controlling into the far-reaching extents
- Ice in the blizzards and ice in the breezes, ice in the solid states and ice in the frozen forms
- Ice in the depths and ice on the ridges, ice in the settled tranquillity and ice in the mystical quiets

- The surface of the earth, with its depths and its heights, with its underneaths and its skies, is replete with one and only the authoritative water
- Salty waters and sweet waters, mineral waters and plain waters
- Liquid waters and solid waters, pliable waters and dense waters
- Cold waters and hot waters, clear waters and coarse waters
- Stream waters and wave-waters, evaporated waters and rain waters
- Water in the storms and water in the floods, water in the living-tissues and water all along

- The sun is keenly monitoring the sedulous planet earth for its progress in the change ensuing in its heart the key to the mind of the solar-system
- Numerous species are either extinct or are on the verge of extiction and the rest are on the mercy of the change
- Impediments, restrictions and confinements are the order of the day for all the activities of the age-old natural-system of the earth
- Be it the oceans or the surface or the mountains or the atmosphere, all the animals be it oceanic or land or winged , be it Paleozoic or Mesozoic or Cenozoic
- Suddenly found themselves into the scourge of the change or the doom of annihilation
- Suddenly the sun has brightened its spectrum of vivid colors celebrating the new born hope for the pinnacle of power and the respendent radiance of the supernatural

- Full scale use and methods for drawing out resources from their dens
- Improving day by day, be it be for water, mineral, fuel and energy, ferrous and non-ferrous metals
- Be it be for many other commodities and resources in liquid, solid or gaseous form
- And still further, planning is on for the start of this process on the moon, may it be to amend its rhythmic metre
- And at the planet mars and other bodies and their sub bodies in the solar-system
- Extending control over their territories and over their destinies

- Full scale use of land and its fertility
- The method are improving day by day, be it be for farming, agriculture and cultivation
- Be it be for food production, husbandry, crofting or rearing of animals
- Be it be for land, water or sea animals, farm-lands or fisheries
- And are reaching to the high points of research and development
- And the taste buds are reaching to the lofty levels, day by day, into the choice relishing

- Full scale use of building and construction
- The methods for shelter, housing, monuments
- Improving day by day, be it be or gardens, walk ways, palaces
- Be it be for residential, commercial or tourism
- Be it be for luxury, comfort, extravagance or relaxation and affluence
- And all-round accomplishment into the movement of scaling new auras and horizons

- Full scale use of motion, energy, fuel and speed
- The methods for movement, gestures, picturesque,composition or telecom
- Improving day by day, be it be for road-carriage, railroad, shipping, airborne carriers
- Be it be for acting, performing,artistry, Motion-pictures
- Be it for passion and enthusiasm or luxury and desire or zeal and objectivity
- And all-round accomplishment into the movement of scaling new auras and horizons

- Full scale use of faiths and beliefs, nationalities and power of dominance, castes and creeds
- Methods improving day by day, be it be for political and social divides, seperiority and assets, creating hegemonies and celebrated conglomerations and for establishing virtual control over beleaguered or corrupt governments and their nations
- Be it be for invincible armed forces and attainment of weapons of mass destruction of atomic or chemical entities and for blatant trade into conventional weapons or medern techniques of annihilation-warheads
- Be it be for hatered-mongers and racial-convenors, prostitution or drug-trafficing, indirect slaveries and terror usurpers
- Be it be over control over one another over creating impediments at migratory routes, over domesticating and using at will the freedom of one and all
- And reaching the state where man finds itself into the dilemma of taking pride into its own perils, into nations and their boundaries, into their divides in every sphere of their indulgence and existence

- At any given time, some entities become fast and furious impositions, other toe the line for survival and sustenance and remaining many are ruined into their precarious condition of suffering and destitution
- Bigotry in faith or nationalism and imbalance into the profiles of the human-race as a whole is the stigma of unsurmountable proportion and mitigation
- Cry for independence is conspicuous by its absence and leanings for freedom from shackles of divides , boundaries and impediments are virtually non-existent
- Will some day, the man will stand up and pay the cost, whatever it may be, to accomplish meaningful freedom and true independence into an integrated world
- Will some day, the man will rise up and break the wall of human-divide, crush the curse of flagrant inhumanity and transform itself into a flawless oneself and chant independence, independence, independence, independence
- Celebrations, jubilations, enchantment and fascination, the cluster of roses and the permeating fragrance in their roseate petals, the charm of finches and the musical demeanour in their lyrical songs

17. CHEW THE CUD - II　　　　(40)

.... THE SUN ....　　　**(8)**

- Effervescent and into a continuous process of giving birth
- To the energy, heat and light being the food for the soul of the almighty
- At the centre of the mammoth revolving and moving spherical heat-ball
- This sun being one of the numerous and endless similar stars housed into the body of the space

- Enlightened and hallowed, vigorous and animated
- Bustling in stupendous energy, flourishing in absolute authority
- Reproach and venom are melted into merciless and brazen fire
- Emphatic and settled, sparkling and scintillating

- Golden gilt, glowing and glittering
- Gleaming and glazing, the grand majesty
- Gilded gem, glaring and glistening
- Glinting and glossing, the glorious meander

- Dreamy outlook, fascinating and mesmerizing
- Beguiling and bewitching, the marvelous magnificence
- Hypnotic charisma, alluring and captivating
- Seducing and enthralling, the fulfilling wondrous silvery moon

- Secure and secluded, smug and complacent
- Genial and contented, elated and rapturous
- Animated and chirpy, buoyant and convivial
- Spirited and bouncy, cheery and jubilant

- Spinning into its revolution, revolving into its orbit
- Invigorating into its sunlight, enlivening into its sun-shine
- Transfixed into its full-moon, bemused into its no-moon
- Exalted into its moon-shine, exhilarated into its moon-light

- From out of no where and not from the apparent universe
- From an inexplicable source and not from the material universe
- From within the eternal transcendence and not from the dazzling cosmos
- From within the space , the infinity itself and not from the resplendent cosmos

- Light in spiritual form struck the planet earth
- Bound it into its total control and tookover its natural- system
- A transient system of change replaced the system of the natural-evolution
- The planet earth becomes an engine of growth for the ensuing change

- The planet earth made the humans its flagship entity
- And ushered in an era of use of mining, energy, motion and technology
- And lured the man to chew the cud and ponder over taste and luxury
- And overusing the natural resources and advancing into their scientific applications

- The earth has adopted the change and thereby is adhering to its new-found aspiration of merging into the sun
- The man has become philosopher and expert in every sphere of skillful activity
- The man has become scientists, explorers and astronauts reaching out to other horizons of their solar-system
- The knowledge is taking shape in full swing in pursuance of the attainment of the goal, the ultimate

18. CHANGEOVER-ANCE - II (40)

.... THE COSMOS .... (20)

- Blistering into the surfeit of intense radiance
- Brimming into the gush of burning brilliance
- Bustling into the plethora of coruscating incandescence
- Blazing into the glut of profound scintillation

- Regulated stars, enormous in their sizes
- Colossal in their extents, gigantic in their magnitudes
- Gargantuan in their dimensions, giant in their massiveness
- Mammoth in their masses, huge in their immensity

- Energy being created ceaselessly at their centres
- Matter flourishing vehemently within their bodies
- Motion regulating wholly the every solar-system
- Gravity controlling meticulously the counterbalance of the whole cosmos

- Relativities being formed throughout the whole of the material-universe
- Between the bodies of all the units of all the solar-systems
- Energy, matter, motion and gravity participating unwittingly
- The true joy being created continuously throughout the whole of the cosmos

- The binary purpose prompted the creation of the material-universe
- To keep fulfilling with true joy the trans-eternal body of bliss
- To keep feeding with energy the permeating and voracious eternal-soul
- The cosmos fulfilling this dual purpose perfectly and uninterruptedly

- The eternal-soul zooming on its energy-consumption
- The eternal body joyous into its infinity and transcendence
- The eternal mind blissful into its trans-eternal creativity
- The event of periodical review of the material universe, embracements and congratulations

- Celebration and jubilation, enchantment and fascination
- Embellishment and enrichment, accretion and accomplishment
- Fulfilment with aphrodisiac, ecstasy and consummation
- Contentment and transcendence, blissful and sublime

- On this auspicious occasion, in this gathering of the divinities
- On this reiteration of the unison, in this meeting of the trans-eternal bodies
- On this conformation of the purity, in this chorus of the eternal entities
- An August gift-the Augmentation of the recipient - is announced

- Amongst the candidates of the short-listed eligibles, the beneficiary being decided in a lottery-draw
- A windfall is beckoning on the horizon, the sun becomes the winner of the covetous award
- Thereby, the sun will reach its ultimate pinnacle, the sun will be transformed into the supernatural star
- The sun chooses the planet earth to lead the change, the earth earnestly accepts the stupendous challenge

- The period of change is on, the schedule of the changeover-ance comes into effect
- The progress into the journey is exhilirating, passing by the grandeurs of the magnificence
- Penetrating deeply into the wonders of the natural-system, crushing recklessly the age-old establishment and its environments
- The covenant of the technocracy is unmistakable, the resplendence of the ascendancy into the realm is inevitable

www.ingramcontent.com/pod-product-compliance
Lightning Source LLC
LaVergne TN
LVHW052035080426
835513LV00018B/2330